WANDERINGS

Brought to you by
Kids' Health Links Foundation (KHLF)

Special thanks to the Upopolis Grief Island Lead: Melissa Dodaro, MSc., CCLS for her work as author and creator.

Thank you to the KHLF team and Betina Sales (Upopolis intern 2023) for their valuable contribution to this notebook. Thank you to our donors for making this possible.

© Kids' Health Links Foundation, 2024
Copy with written permission only

A Wayfinder's Grief Notebook.

Wanderings

Copyright © 2024 by Kids' Health Links Foundation

All rights reserved. No part of this publication may be reproduced, distributed, or transmitted in any form or by any means, including photocopying, recording, or other electronic or mechanical methods, without the prior written permission of the author, except in the case of brief quotations embodied in critical reviews and certain other non-commercial uses permitted by copyright law.

ISBN 978-1-7796-2138-2 (Paperback)

WHAT'S IN THE GRIEF Notebook?

Intro
- How to use this notebook
- Why journal?
- Introductory materials

Wonders
- Common questions about grief
- Grief Dictionary
- Feelings Dictionary
- Guided journal activities

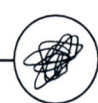

Worries
- Reflection exercises
- Guided journal activities
- Coping strategies

Wayfinding
- Guided journal activities, strategies, and exercises to support you as you navigate your grief

Wishes
- Continuing bonds activities
- Focused journal prompts
- Goal setting
- Expressing yourself

HOW TO USE THIS GRIEF Notebook?

START HERE!

DECORATE AND DOODLE

Design the cover page with doodles, images, words, stickers, and more. This notebook is a creative opportunity for you to express yourself! Be creative and make each page your own.

JOURNAL ANY WAY

We made this notebook for grieving youth. Some parts might feel useful for you, while other parts might not, and that is okay. Do what feels right to you – work from front to back or jump around to parts you choose.

LET YOUR THOUGHTS FLOW
there's no right or wrong way to journal

SHARE AND CONNECT

Sometimes it is hard to know how you feel until you express it. Once you do, you might have different questions, feelings, and ideas that might require the support of a trusting adult to help you navigate. Use the notebook to guide and support those conversations.

PURPOSEFUL PAUSE

Throughout the notebook, you will encounter purposeful pauses. A purposeful pause is an opportunity to take a break where you can stop journaling for a moment, take a deep breath, and learn new information that is interesting, easy to remember, and empowering.

The goal of each purposeful pause is to promote reflection and growth, while encouraging you to consider different views and approaches, to help you on your grief journey.

WHY

EXPRESS YOUR EMOTIONS

Sometimes, it's hard to put into words how you're feeling. Journaling provides a safe space to express yourself honestly and without judgment.

UNDERSTANDING YOURSELF

Gain insights into your thoughts, feelings and emotions. Journaling is a way to get to know yourself better during a challenging time and see your growth overtime.

REMEMBER AND HONOUR

Choose to cherish and remember the person or people who have died by documenting special memories, stories, and moments that you want to hold onto.

RELEASE AND RELIEF

Putting pen to paper can provide a sense of release. It's like taking a weight off your shoulders. It can help you process feelings and find moments of peace and calm.

CONNECTING WITH OTHERS

Your notebook is a private space, but it can also be a bridge to connect with others. Sharing your thoughts with a trusted friend or family member can be a powerful way to strengthen your support system.

All About U

This notebook belongs to: _____

I am _____ years old.

This year, I want to: _____

A fun fact about me: _____

A favourite memory: _____

My Self Portrait!

My top 5 favorite interests are:

1. _____
2. _____
3. _____
4. _____
5. _____

I am good at:

My support people are:

My goals for the future are: _____

"Sometimes, the smallest step in the right direction ends up being the biggest step of your life. Tiptoe if you must, but take a step."
- Naeem Callaway

WONDERS

QUESTIONS • THOUGHTS • FEELINGS
CURIOSITIES

WONDERS

IN THIS SECTION, YOU CAN...

- **Learn about the 6 C's which are common questions or concerns you may have**
  (page 12-13)

- **Explore the Grief Dictionary and Feelings Dictionary**
  (page 14-18)

- **Write, draw & think about your wonders as you engage in guided journal activities**
  (page 19-25)

WHAT YOU MIGHT NEED

Pencil or Pen

Coloured Pencils

Mindful Breaks

COMMON QUESTIONS

The 6 C's OF GRIEF

WHAT IS IT CALLED?
Grief! Grief is a normal response to any loss, including death and non-death specific loss, and includes all the thoughts, feelings, emotions, and reactions we have.

CAN I CATCH IT?
No. Grief is not something that can be "caught" like an infection or virus. It is a response you have to loss. However, when someone we know is grieving, we may feel empathy in response to their emotions, but this is a natural and normal response to human connection and is not the same as "catching" grief itself.

DID I CAUSE IT?
You did not cause your grief. It is common for grieving youth to experience feelings of guilt or self-blame, even when they have not done anything wrong. Know that your feelings are normal and your grief is not something you caused or could have prevented. It is important to be gentle with yourself and know that you are worthy of love and support.

COMMON QUESTIONS
The 6 C's
OF GRIEF

CAN I CURE IT?
Grief can't be fixed or eliminated; it becomes a natural part of you. While it's normal to wish for its disappearance, this is not possible. Over time, you will grow around your grief. It will remain a part of you, but you will also have new experiences and moments of joy alongside it.

WHO WILL TAKE CARE OF ME?
You're surrounded by a supportive network of people who care about you, including family, friends, teachers, counselors, and community organizations. Reaching out to those you trust can help you feel seen, heard, and supported during your grief. Remember, you're never alone, even when it may feel that way.

HOW CAN I STAY CONNECTED?
You have the power to decide how to stay connected to the person who died. Whether it's through physical objects, spiritual practices, symbolic gestures, or rituals, it's your choice. There's no right or wrong way, so explore what feels most meaningful and comforting to you.

GRIEF

Anticipatory Grief (noun):
Grief feelings that occur before an event (death or loss) happen.

Bereavement (noun):
A time of mourning after someone has died.

Coping (verb/noun):
The different skills, strategies, and activities people use to handle their thoughts and feelings when they are experiencing something new, challenging, or unexpected.

Dead (adjective):
When a body has stopped working and will never work again. The body cannot move, breathe, think, feel, see, smell, or talk. The body does not feel pain, hunger, or fear.

Dying (verb):
A natural part and process of life where living things die. Sometimes it happens quickly and sometimes it happens slowly over time.

Grief (noun):
A normal response to any loss (for example, death and non-death-specific loss) and includes all the thoughts, feelings, emotions, and reactions.

Loss (noun):
The fact or process of losing someone or something. This can include death as well as non-death specific loss. Non-death specific loss can include moving schools, separation, parental divorce, injury or illness leading to changes in functioning, distance between friends or family members, etc.

GRIEF Dictionary

MAiD (noun):
In some countries, when someone has an illness that will cause their body to die, they can ask a doctor to help their body die. The doctor uses medication that stops the body from working. This is done in a way that is not painful. In Canada, this is called medical assistance in dying, or MAiD.

Mourning (noun):
The outward expression of grief.

Murder (noun):
When someone ends someone else's life and causes their body to die.

Overdose (noun):
When someone accidently or on purpose, takes too much of a substance and it affects their body's ability to work properly. This can cause the person's body to die.

Trigger (noun):
Anything that can bring back strong thoughts, feelings, and reminders of an experience or event that can cause big feelings, such as overwhelm, sadness, or anger. Some triggers can include, smells, pictures, songs, movies, events, and more!

Stressor (noun):
External and internal factors that can make people feel stressed or worried. Common external stressors include changes in daily routines, illness or injury, school/exams, or the holiday season. Common internal stressors include wanting to do well in school or fit in with peers, feelings of anxiety, fear, or anger.

Suicide (noun):
When a person causes his/her/their body to stop working; the body dies.

FEELINGS Dictionary

ANGRY
When something does not go your way, you don't understand something, or you can't control, change, or fix something.

EMBARRASSED
When you are self-conscious, confused, and upset about experiencing something new, or having people see you or talk about you in a way that makes you feel uncomfortable.

ANXIOUS
When you are worried or nervous because you don't know what to expect, you're not sure if you are safe, or you are in a situation that is stressful.

EXCITED
When you are thinking about something pleasant or thrilling that is going to happen, doing something that makes you feel good, or seeing someone important to you.

CALM
When you feel relaxed and peaceful, or when your mind and body are focused and still.

FRUSTRATED
When you are upset about something changing or not going your way, when you can't control, change, or fix something, or when you are not able to achieve something alone and need help to accomplish that thing.

CONFUSED
When you are unsure of how to feel or what to do about something, or when you are given information that is hard to understand or unclear.

GRATEFUL
When you feel thankful for something and focus on the good things in your life.

CURIOUS
When you are interested in learning or understanding something new or unfamiliar.

GUILTY
When you feel responsible for something hard or sad that happened.

FEELINGS Dictionary

HAPPY
When you're having a good time, doing things you enjoy, or with people you enjoy being with.

HELPLESS
When you are not able to help someone or fix something that is important to you, when you feel you can't stand up for yourself and what you believe in, or when you feel powerless.

HOPEFUL
When you are optimistic or positive about something good happening in the future, like getting to do something you want to do or feeling happiness.

JEALOUS
When you can't do or have something that someone else can, like your friends having two living parents.

LONELY
When you feel left out, alone with your thoughts or worries, or feel like you don't belong.

OVERWHELMED
When you have lots of tasks to complete and not enough time to get everything done, or when your mind is racing with thoughts and worries that you can't change, control, or deal with.

SAD
When things that you want to stay the same, change, when you experience any type of loss in life, or when you are unhappy.

SCARED
When you feel afraid of something real, pretend, or unknown.

SURPRISED
When something unexpected, shocking, or sudden happens in a good way or a bad way.

TIRED
When your mind and body have low energy and are in need of rest or sleep.

PURPOSEFUL PAUSE

The feelings dictionary is a list of feelings that you can explore and refer back to at any time. When exploring the feelings dictionary, you might realize that you have some feelings and not others. Some feelings might only last for a moment and other times, they last a little longer. You might feel one or more feelings at the same time. Some might feel easy, while others might feel hard and heavy. Take the time to explore each feeling and reflect on which ones you feel most often.

It is important to remember that feelings are a normal part of life, and they are a part of everyone. Any and every feeling you have is valid, important and normal! When we are able to recognize and identify our feelings, then we are better able to support our minds and bodies and cope with the twists and turns of life.

I ALSO FEEL

What are other feelings that you have felt that are not included in the feelings dictionary? List or draw them out.

FEEL IT OUT

It is normal to have lots of different feelings at different times. Feelings can look and feel different in our minds and bodies too! Wonder about how grief feels in your body and remember, this may change day-by-day or overtime. Here are some places you might feel grief in your body.

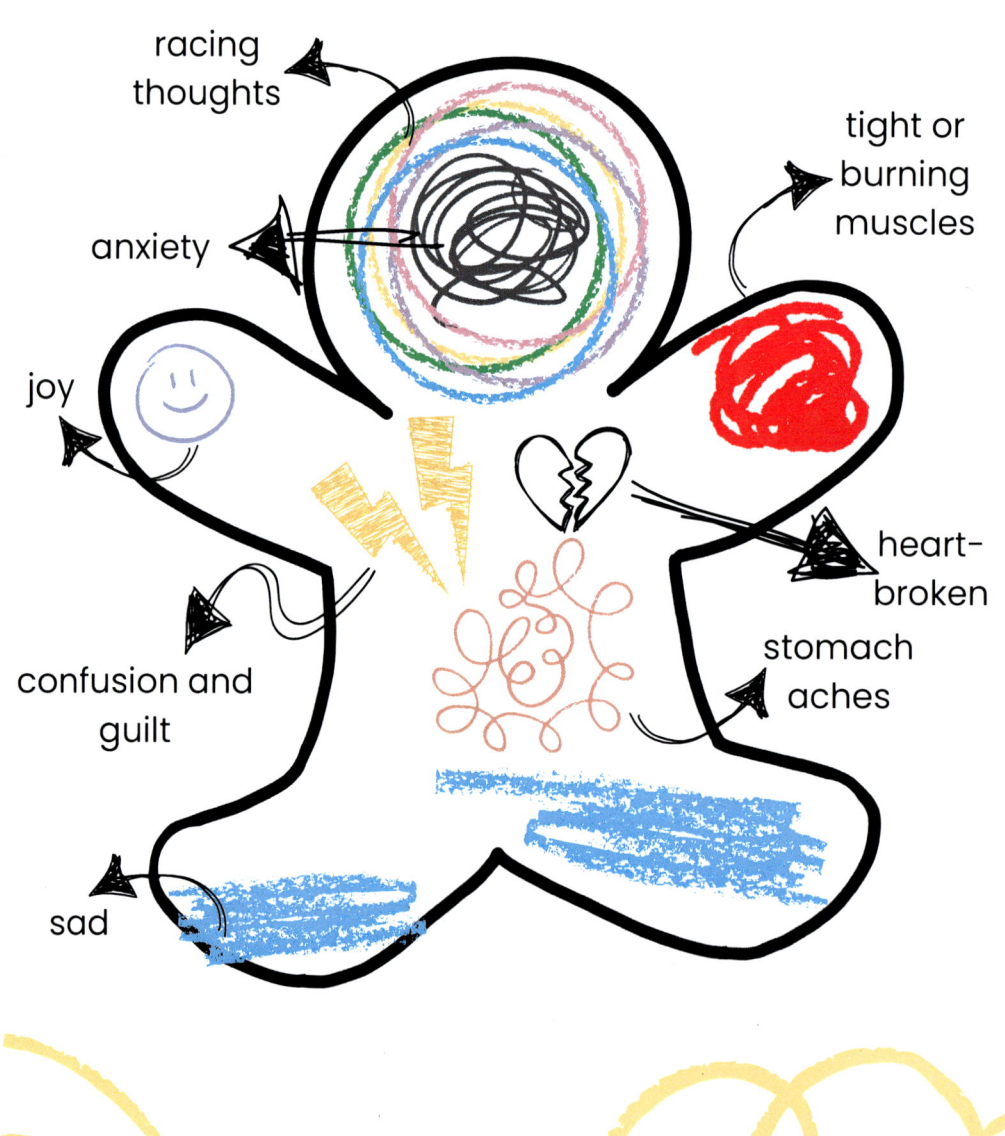

FEEL IT OUT

For this exercise, think about where you are in your grief journey, and express how grief feels or shows up in your body. You can use colours, shapes, words, scribbles, and more!

I WONDER...

Is there anything you're wondering about grief? Use this space to express your wonders, thoughts, and questions.

If there are questions that people have asked you that you don't know how to answer, you can put them here too! Who might be able to answer them? You can put their name beside the question and ask them to help!

PURPOSEFUL PAUSE

It is important to recognize, understand, name, and manage our feelings.

When we start by naming our feelings, we have the power to "tame" them and become less reactive. Dr. Dan Siegel, author of The Whole Brain Child, explains that when we identify how we are feeling by naming the emotion, we validate and normalize our experiences and how we are feeling, which has a "taming" effect. Once we label our emotions we can find healthy solutions to cope with them, creating a calmer mind and body.

I NOTICE, I FEEL, I CAN

Here is a three step exercise that can help with managing big feelings. First, pause and notice how feelings show up and feel in your body. Then, identify the feeling by naming it. Finally, choose a strategy to manage the feeling you identified. Try this exercise to help manage big feelings.

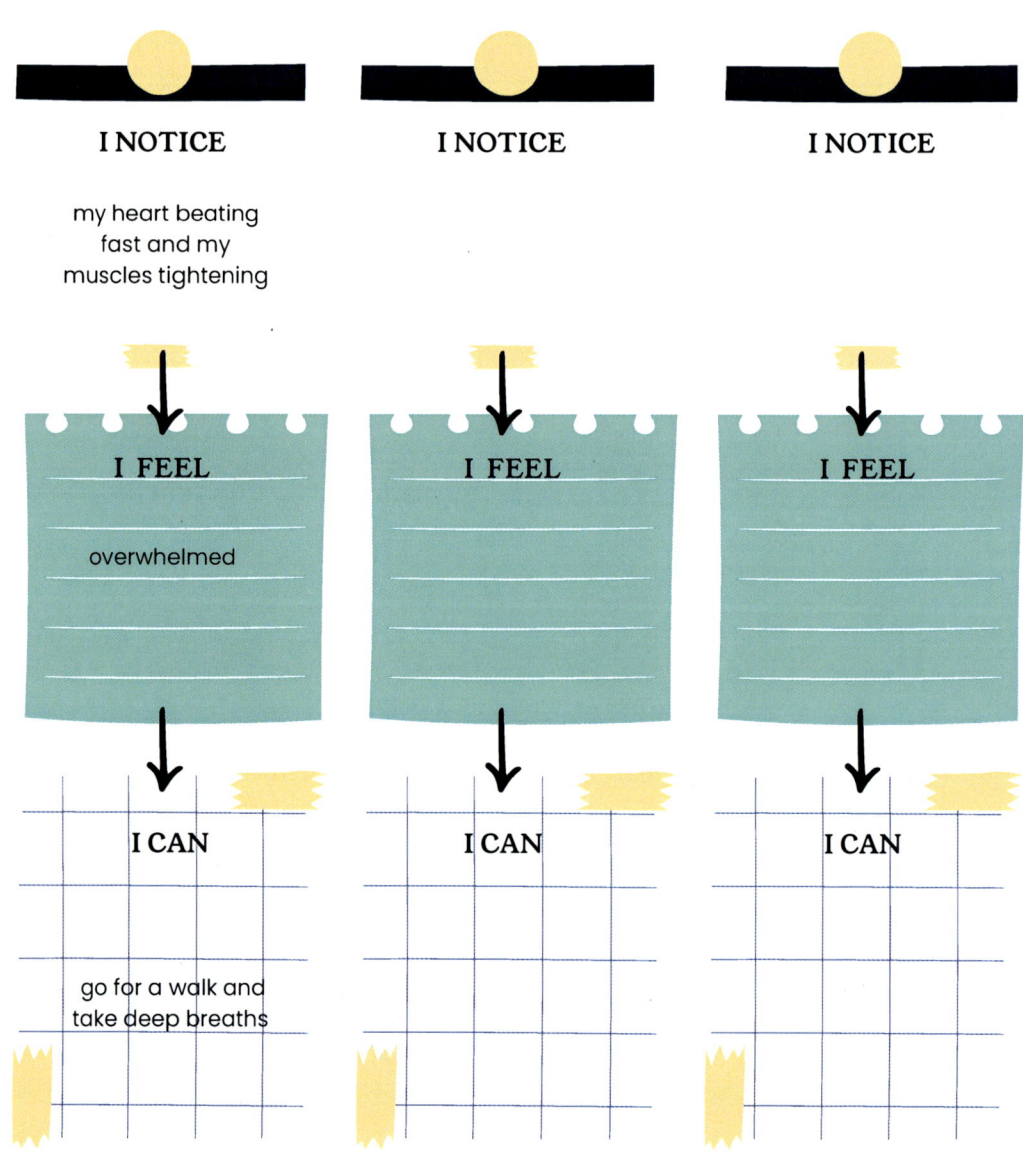

I NOTICE, I FEEL, I CAN

Continue this exercise. Remember, when you take the time to notice and identify your feelings, you can make healthy choices to support your coping!

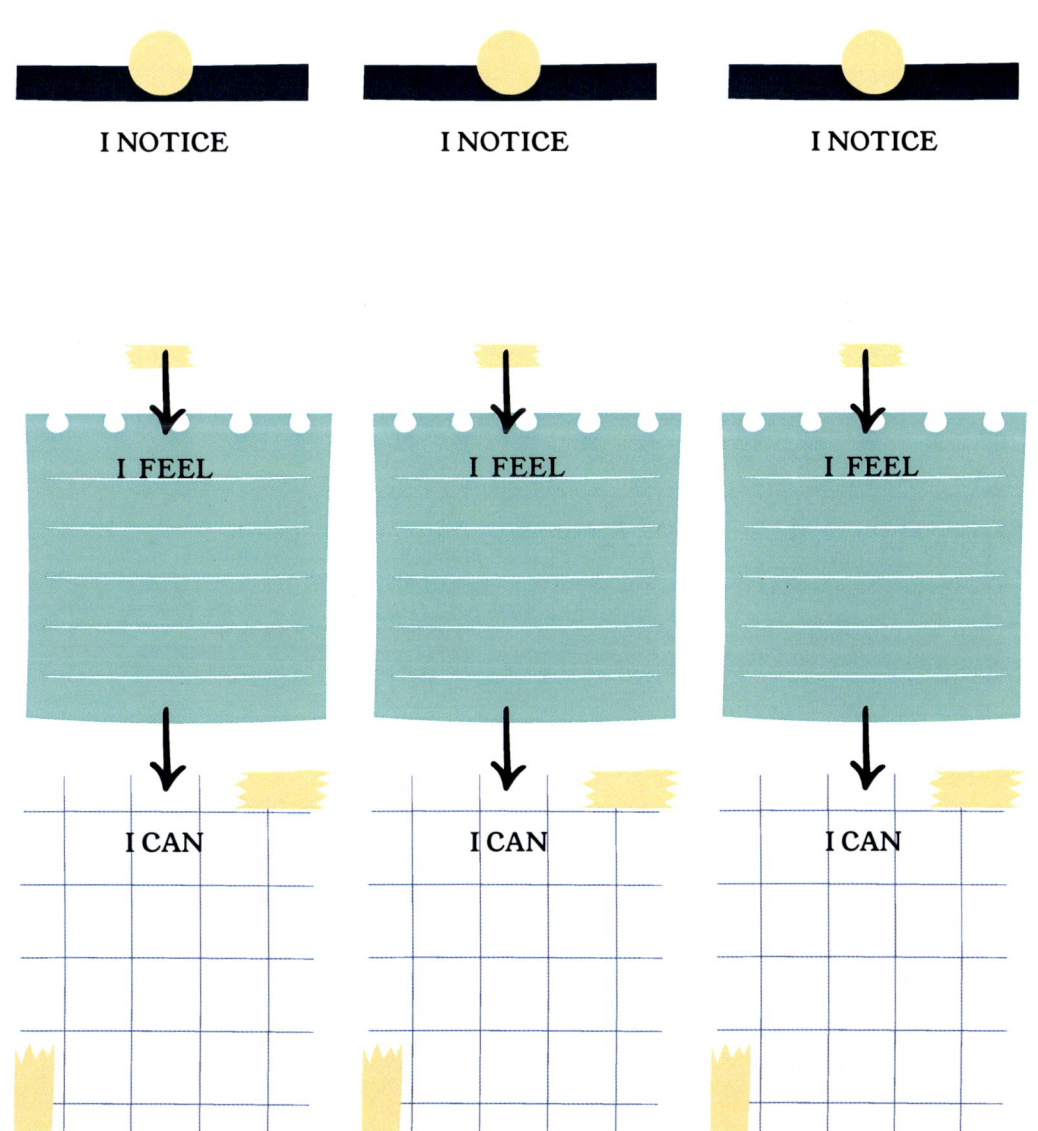

WORRIES
THOUGHTS • FEELINGS
UNCERTAINTIES

WORRIES

IN THIS SECTION, YOU CAN...

- Practice self-reflection and explore your emotions

  (page 28-35)

- Learn new coping skills that you can use throughout the week

  (page 37)

- Process and understand your thoughts, feelings, and coping strategies

  (page 38-41)

WHAT YOU MIGHT NEED

 **Pencil or Pen**

 **Coloured Pencils**

 **Mindful Breaks**

WRITE IT OUT

Notice your worry, find the words to describe it, identify helpful strategies to handle it, and focus on what might happen if your worry does not come true.

WHAT AM I WORRIED ABOUT?
_____
_____
_____
_____
_____

HOW DOES THIS WORRY MAKE ME FEEL?

WHAT MIGHT HAPPEN IF MY WORRY DOES NOT COME TRUE? THINK OF A POSITIVE OUTCOME.
_____
_____
_____
_____
_____
_____
_____
_____

WHAT COPING STRATEGIES WILL I USE TO HANDLE MY WORRY?
☐ _____
☐ _____
☐ _____
☐ _____
☐ _____
☐ _____
☐ _____
☐ _____
☐ _____

EXAMPLES ON PAGE 37

I AM GRATEFUL FOR?
_____

IF I COULD SAY ONE THING TO MY WORRY IT WOULD BE:

AFTER WRITING OUT MY WORRY, I FEEL:
_____

DATE:

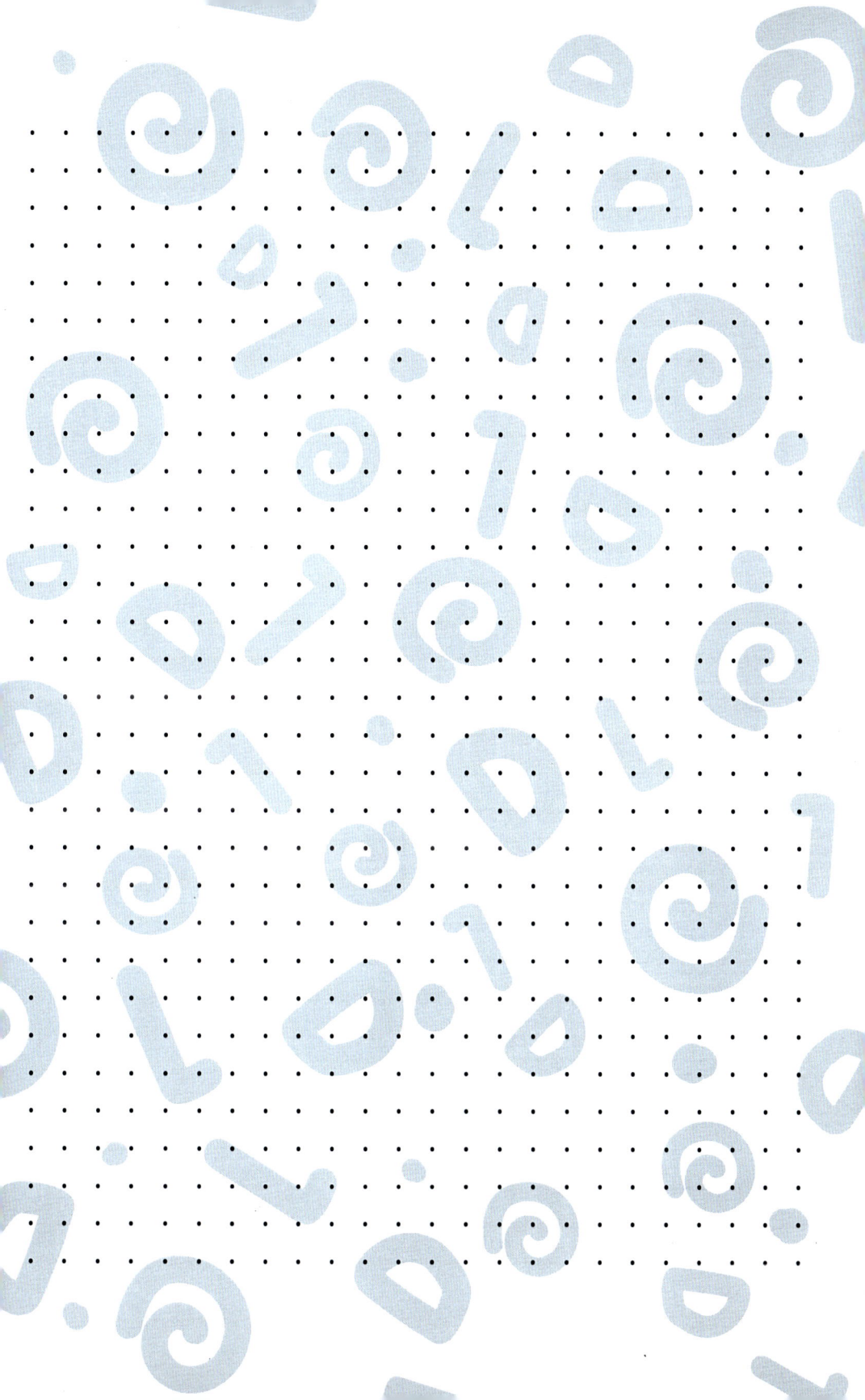

WRITE IT OUT

Notice your worry, find the words to describe it, identify helpful strategies to handle it, and focus on what might happen if your worry does not come true.

WHAT AM I WORRIED ABOUT?
_____
_____
_____
_____
_____

HOW DOES THIS WORRY MAKE ME FEEL?

😍 😁 😑 🙁 😢 😤

WHAT MIGHT HAPPEN IF MY WORRY DOES NOT COME TRUE? THINK OF A POSITIVE OUTCOME.
_____
_____
_____
_____
_____
_____
_____
_____

WHAT COPING STRATEGIES WILL I USE TO HANDLE MY WORRY?
☐ _____
☐ _____
☐ _____
☐ _____
☐ _____
☐ _____
☐ _____
☐ _____
☐ _____

EXAMPLES ON PAGE 37

I AM GRATEFUL FOR?

IF I COULD SAY ONE THING TO MY WORRY IT WOULD BE:

AFTER WRITING OUT MY WORRY, I FEEL:
_____

DATE:

WRITE IT OUT

Notice your worry, find the words to describe it, identify helpful strategies to handle it, and focus on what might happen if your worry does not come true.

WHAT AM I WORRIED ABOUT?
_____
_____
_____
_____
_____

HOW DOES THIS WORRY MAKE ME FEEL?
😍 😁 😐 🙁 😢 😤

WHAT MIGHT HAPPEN IF MY WORRY DOES NOT COME TRUE? THINK OF A POSITIVE OUTCOME.
_____
_____
_____
_____
_____
_____
_____
_____

WHAT COPING STRATEGIES WILL I USE TO HANDLE MY WORRY?
- [ ] _____
- [ ] _____
- [ ] _____
- [ ] _____
- [ ] _____
- [ ] _____
- [ ] _____
- [ ] _____
- [ ] _____

EXAMPLES ON PAGE 37

I AM GRATEFUL FOR?

IF I COULD SAY ONE THING TO MY WORRY IT WOULD BE:

AFTER WRITING OUT MY WORRY, I FEEL:
_____

DATE:

WRITE IT OUT

Notice your worry, find the words to describe it, identify helpful strategies to handle it, and focus on what might happen if your worry does not come true.

WHAT AM I WORRIED ABOUT?
_____
_____
_____
_____
_____

HOW DOES THIS WORRY MAKE ME FEEL?

WHAT COPING STRATEGIES WILL I USE TO HANDLE MY WORRY?
- [ ] _____
- [ ] _____
- [ ] _____
- [ ] _____
- [ ] _____
- [ ] _____
- [ ] _____
- [ ] _____
- [ ] _____

EXAMPLES ON PAGE 37

WHAT MIGHT HAPPEN IF MY WORRY DOES NOT COME TRUE? THINK OF A POSITIVE OUTCOME.
_____
_____
_____
_____
_____
_____
_____
_____

I AM GRATEFUL FOR?

IF I COULD SAY ONE THING TO MY WORRY IT WOULD BE:

AFTER WRITING OUT MY WORRY, I FEEL:
_____

DATE:

PURPOSEFUL PAUSE

We all process our grief differently. For some, it's a thinking process where for others, it's a feeling process and for some, it's a mix of both. Regardless of how you process your grief, worry is a natural response that is both a thinking and feeling process. Worrying is a way of thinking ahead about what might happen. This can cause our bodies to feel nervous, stressed, and overwhelmed.

When we worry, we tend to imagine the worst thing that could happen. As real and hard as these worries feel, it is important to remember that what could happen isn't always the same as what will happen. If something is worrying you, it helps to notice the worry, find the words to describe it, identify helpful strategies to handle it (including gratitude), and focus on positive outcomes. It's normal to worry but if you find you are worrying too much, talking to a trusting adult and getting the right help can be a big relief.

DAILY COPING IDEAS

Mindful Monday
Ground yourself: Name 5 things you see, 4 things you feel, 3 things you hear, 2 things you smell & 1 thing you taste

Take Care of U Tuesday
Move your body in ways that feel good to release physical tension and improve your mood

Way Back Wednesday
Engage in creative activities like drawing, painting, writing, or crafting. Let your imagination soar

Thankful Thursday
Keep a gratitude jar where you write down things you are thankful for and place them in the jar

Feel-Good Friday
Create a playlist of songs that make you feel good and energized. Listen to this playlist on repeat and dance it out!

Social Saturday
Reach out to friends, family, or trusted community members to share your thoughts and feelings

Self-Care Sunday
Create a calming space with a bubble bath or a long shower. Personal grooming is important and soothing

Affirmations
- I am growing and learning every day
- I deserve kindness and compassion
- I am worthy of love and respect
- I believe in my abilities and potential

WORRY MAP

Where do your worries come from? Create a map of worries that come from different areas in your life (examples: "Homework Hill", "BFF Bay", "Home"). Like using a map to navigate, creating a worry map can help you organize your worries, identify triggers, and plan supportive strategies to use to improve your coping.

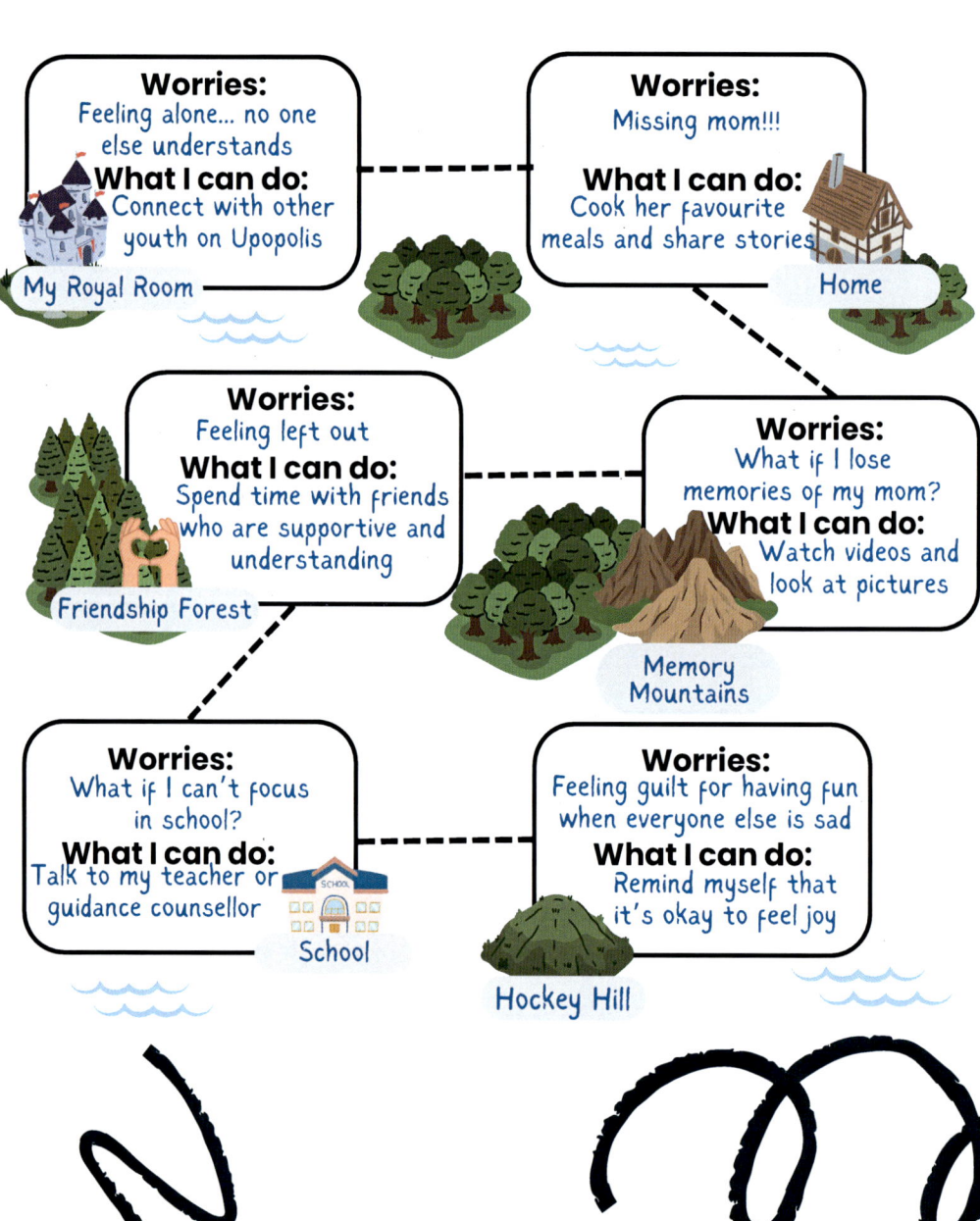

WORRY MAP

For this exercise, map out your worries. Reflect on and identify what places and spaces your worries exist within. Do you notice any patterns or environments where you have more or less worries? Where do you feel safest?

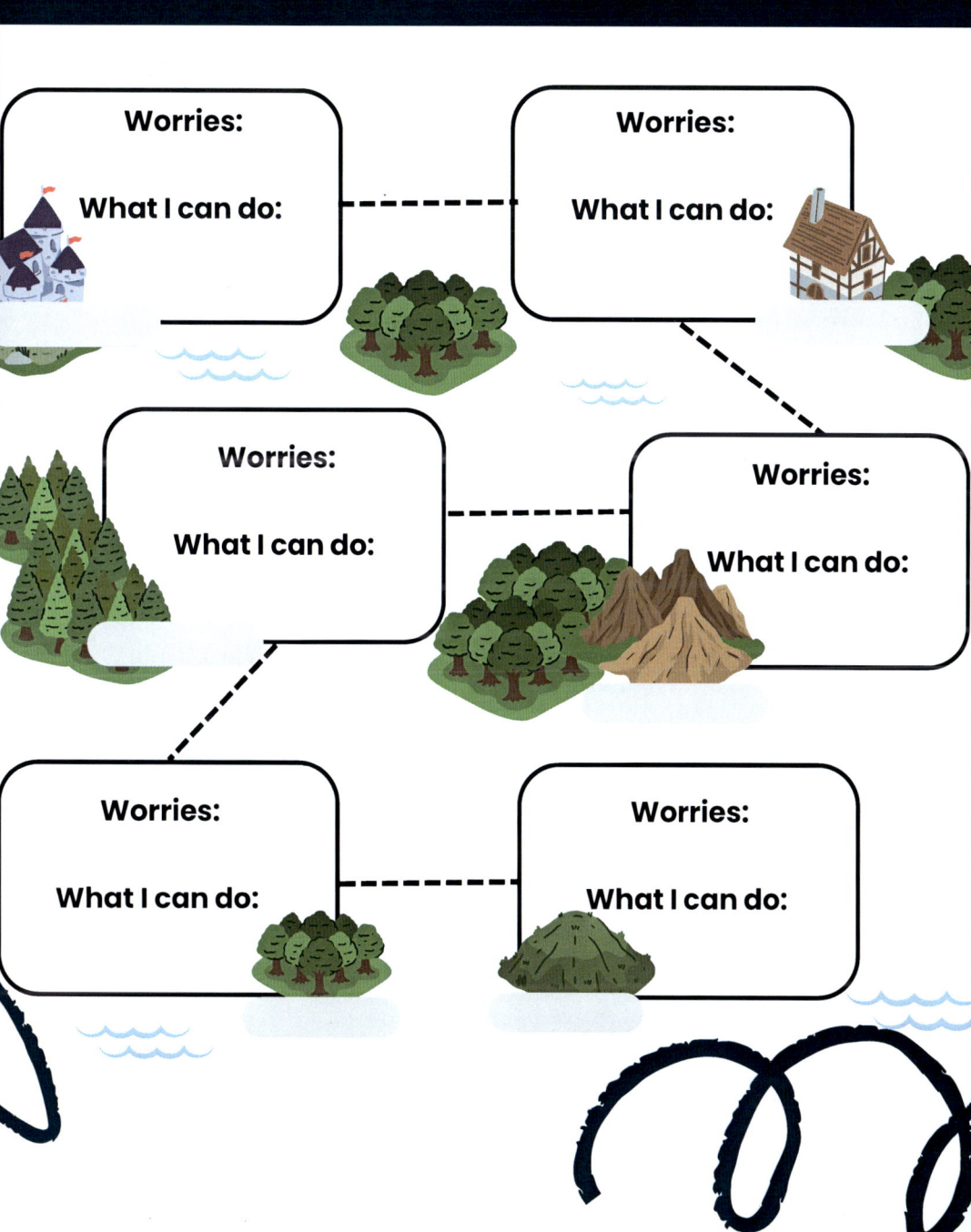

BE RIGHT BACK BOXES

Inside each box, write one question or worry you have. Imagine closing your worry inside the box. You can open each box when you have more time, strategies, and supports (like trusting adults) to help you handle the worry inside. Don't forget to date your boxes. When you re-open them, think about if these worries still exists or it they have changed?

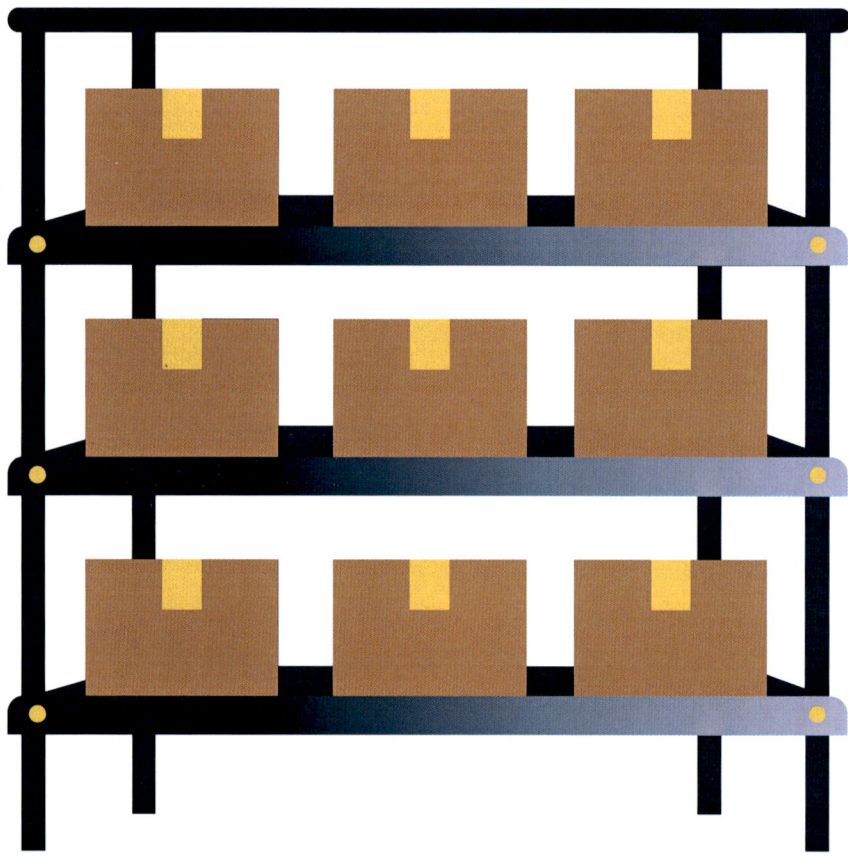

This exercise is called compartmentalizing. It is a useful technique that can help you manage worries. When we have lots of thoughts/worries in our mind, it can be easy to think about the "what ifs". This visualization exercise invites you to identify the worries taking up space in your mind so you feel less overwhelmed. Doing this also makes room for other emotions and experiences. Return to your shelf as needed.

HELPFUL vs. UNHELPFUL COPING STRATEGIES

Brainstorm coping strategies that you use to manage your big feelings and sort them into the categories below. Use this exercise to reflect on your current strategies as well as to identify new ones.

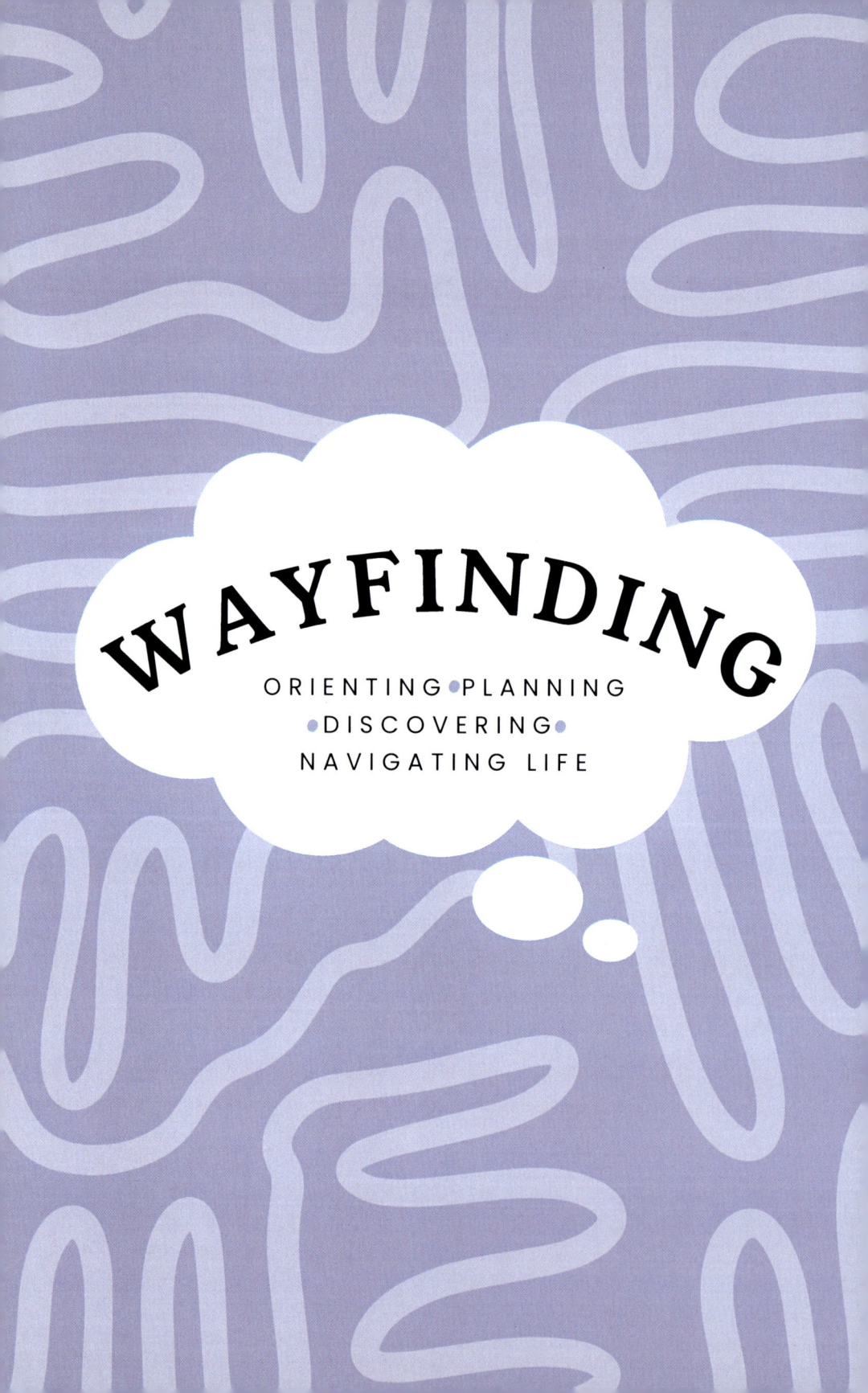

WAYFINDING

IN THIS SECTION, YOU CAN...

Engage in a variety of guided journal activities and exercises that encourage self-reflection, strengthen your expression of gratitude, promote self-discovery, establish boundaries, and support healthy coping

(page 44-69)

WHAT YOU MIGHT NEED

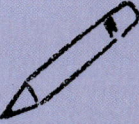 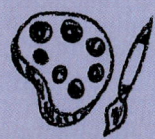  

Pencil or Pen   **Coloured Pencils**   **Craft Materials**   **Mindful Breaks**

GETTING TO KNOW MYSELF

Knowing yourself is important; it can help you be more comfortable with who you are, trust yourself more, know what you need to cope effectively, recognize your strengths and weaknesses, seek support that is appropriate for your needs, and continue to grow and bloom. Fill out the boxes below and get to know yourself better!

PERMISSION PASSES

This is your reminder to give yourself permission to take a break WHENEVER you need one and do things that nourish, refresh, and recharge your mind and body. For example, you can give yourself permission to: go to bed early, take a brain break from social media, or say "no". What will you give yourself permission for? Write one permission in each ticket and use them as needed!

I GIVE MYSELF PERMISSION TO:

NO EXPIRATION DATE

I GIVE MYSELF PERMISSION TO:

NO EXPIRATION DATE

I GIVE MYSELF PERMISSION TO:

NO EXPIRATION DATE

I GIVE MYSELF PERMISSION TO:

NO EXPIRATION DATE

I GIVE MYSELF PERMISSION TO:

NO EXPIRATION DATE

I GIVE MYSELF PERMISSION TO:

NO EXPIRATION DATE

I GIVE MYSELF PERMISSION TO:

NO EXPIRATION DATE

I GIVE MYSELF PERMISSION TO:

NO EXPIRATION DATE

Getting to Know Grief

GROWING AROUND GRIEF

Did you know that you grow around grief? The grief you experience and feel does not get smaller over time, instead, you get bigger and stronger!

GRIEF BURSTS

Sometimes, you can hit up against grief and it can feel really big and hard. This is called a "grief burst". Here are some examples of grief bursts:
- Hearing a song
- Eating a special meal
- Celebrating a holiday

GRIEF GROWTH

On your grief journey, you will also come to find unexpected strength and wisdom, leading to personal growth and moments of positivity. Here are some examples of "grief growth":
- Strengthening relationships and connections
- Understanding your emotions
- Increasing gratitude
- Learning important lessons

GRIEF BURSTS

In this exercise, reflect on and identify times when your grief feels really big as well as ways you have grown. Need help with ideas? Try asking friends or family members.

POSITIVE AFFIRMATIONS

Positive affirmations are short and simple statements that are intentionally repeated to oneself. They can be a positive tool for promoting self-esteem, building confidence and encouraging resilience. For this exercise, find the positive affirmations in the crossword puzzle.

```
I  M  A  T  T  E  R  S  T  M  A  C
E  I  A  M  H  E  L  P  F  U  L  O
I  A  M  E  N  O  U  G  H  A  X  O
A  M  C  O  N  F  I  D  E  N  T  L
M  L  I  A  M  C  A  P  A  B  L  E
G  O  S  G  R  A  T  E  F  U  L  D
O  V  I  A  M  W  O  R  T  H  Y  E
O  E  A  D  S  U  P  P  O  R  T  T
D  D  S  S  I  A  M  S  M  A  R  T
U  E  W  I  A  M  S  T  R  O  N  G
I  A  M  S  P  E  C  I  A  L  M  X
S  I  A  W  E  S  O  M  E  R  T  E
```

I MATTER   I AM GOOD
I AM ENOUGH   I AM HELPFUL
I AM WORTHY   I AM CAPABLE
I AM STRONG   I AM SPECIAL
I AM LOVED   I AM SMART

Once you have found them all, try to incorporate these positive affirmations, as well as others, into your daily routine to promote self-love and healthy coping – your mind and body will thank you!

PURPOSEFUL PAUSE

Knowing what to say to your friends, teachers, classmates, neighbours, and other people in your life can be difficult, especially when we have strong emotions attached to our thoughts and experiences. Creating scripts is one helpful strategy that you can use to practice knowing what to say. Your scripts also sound different depending on WHO you are talking to and they can change anytime... even in the middle of the conversation!

Explore how you will respond *if* or *when* someone asks about the death of someone in your life. Develop the language to use and a simple script so you feel confident and prepared. Remember, you always have permission to share as much or as little of your story, or nothing at all. You are in control. You get to decide.

DEVELOPING MY STORY

Explore this sample script. Then, plan, write and practice your own scripts. Consider how your scripts and the language you use may change when you talk to different people.

When someone asks about what happened, I might say:

My dad died.

Check It Out

When someone asks how my person died, I might say:

My dad died by suicide. This means he caused his body to stop working. My family and I loved my dad and I know he loved us too.

When I want to talk about my person I might say:

My dad was so much fun to be around. He always made me laugh and liked going for walks with me. I feel sad that he is not alive. Sharing stories about him helps me to remember him.

When I want to politely shut down a conversation I can say:

Thank you for talking to me about my dad, but I don't want to continue this conversation today.
OR
I don't feel like sharing right now. Can we talk about something else?

DEVELOPING MY STORY

When someone asks about what happened, I might say:

When I want to talk about my person I might say:

When someone asks how my person died, I might say:

When I want to politely shut down a conversation I can say:

DEVELOPING MY STORY

DEVELOPING MY STORY

When someone asks about what happened, I might say:

When I want to talk about my person I might say:

When someone asks how my person died, I might say:

When I want to politely shut down a conversation I can say:

COPING STRATEGIES

Explore this page and learn about strategies you can use to help your mind and body feel calm.

 Listening to music

 Breathing deeply

Drawing or painting

Reading

 Dancing

 Drinking tea

 Walking

 Listening to nature

 Writing positive Affirmations

 Talking to family

 Quality time with friends

 Moving your body

 Gentle stretching

 Organizing your space

 Jounraling

 Watching a movie

WHAT WORKS FOR ME

People cope in different ways. It takes time to figure out which coping strategies work best for you. On the coping cards below, identify the strategies you might find helpful for when you feel different emotions. Refer back to the Feelings Dictionary if needed.

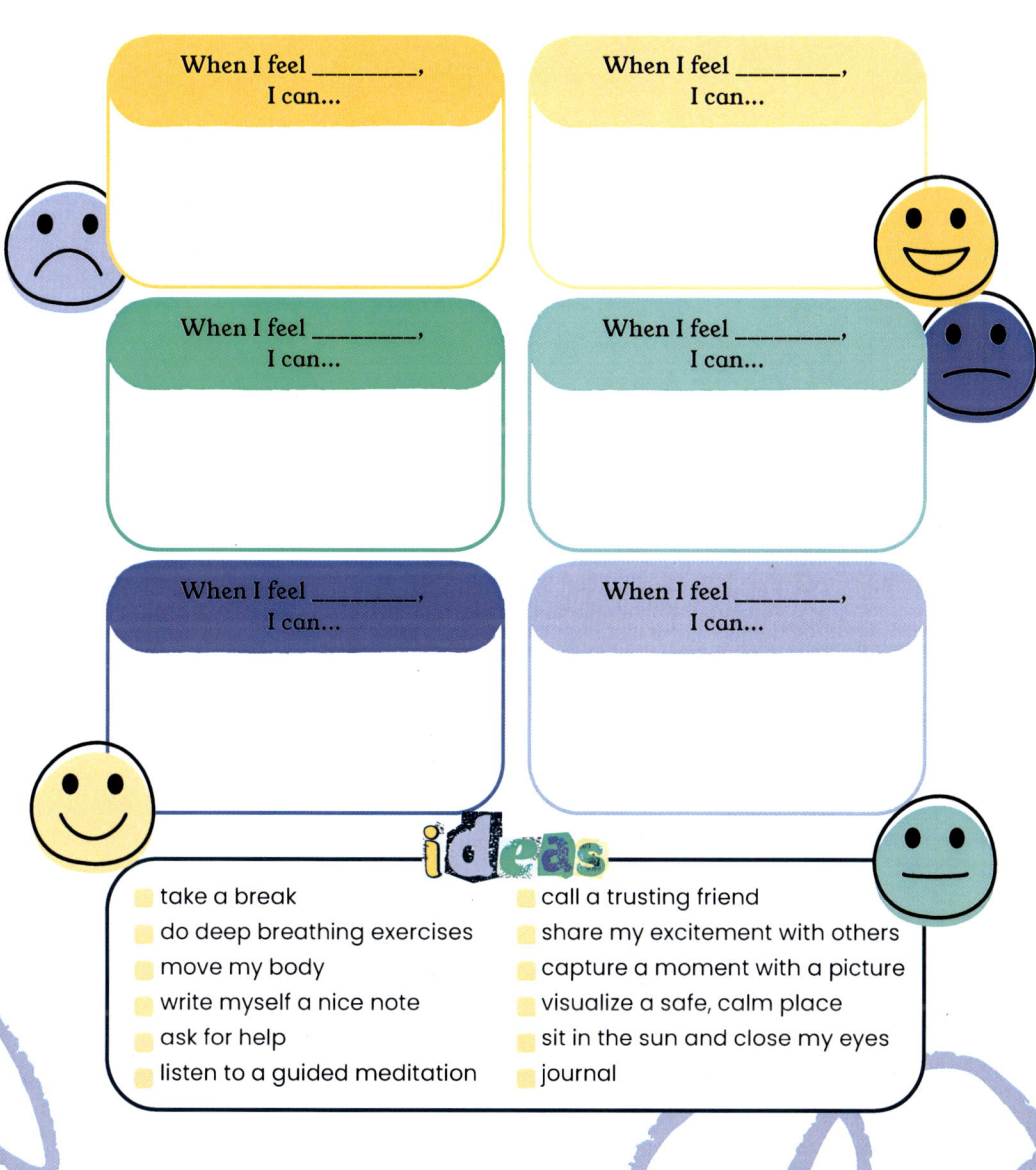

When I feel _____, I can...

When I feel _____, I can...

When I feel _____, I can...

When I feel _____, I can...

When I feel _____, I can...

When I feel _____, I can...

ideas

- take a break
- do deep breathing exercises
- move my body
- write myself a nice note
- ask for help
- listen to a guided meditation
- call a trusting friend
- share my excitement with others
- capture a moment with a picture
- visualize a safe, calm place
- sit in the sun and close my eyes
- journal

PURPOSEFUL PAUSE

Gratitude is when you feel thankful for the good, important, and meaningful things in your life. Gratitude is taking a purposeful pause to reflect on and appreciate the small and big things you have and get to experience, such as the sun on your face, a clear blue sky, or a delicious snack.

Practicing gratitude is important because it increases positive emotions and can support our minds and bodies. Gratitude can help us learn, make smart decisions, balance out hard feelings, build strong relationships, and engage in caring actions (towards self and others).

Make it a habit to pause each day to notice and appreciate what's good in your life... and don't forget to notice and absorb that good feeling that comes with practicing gratitude.

GRATITUDE

Take a mindful pause to notice and appreciate what's good in your life. Repeat this practice daily.

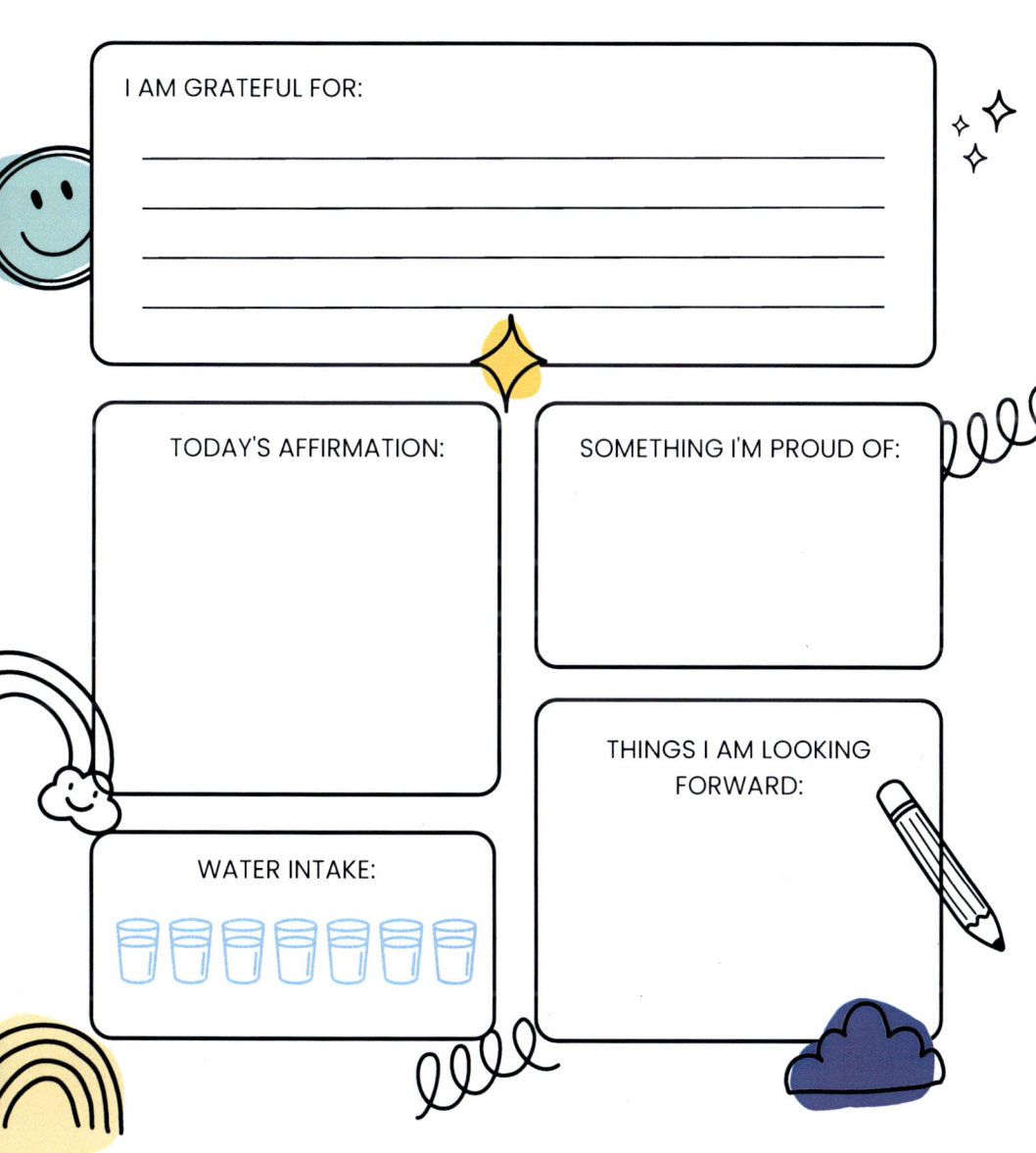

I AM GRATEFUL FOR:
_____
_____
_____
_____

TODAY'S AFFIRMATION:

SOMETHING I'M PROUD OF:

THINGS I AM LOOKING FORWARD:

WATER INTAKE:

ENJOY THE LITTLE THINGS

Life's little joys have the power to fill us with happiness and offer us moments of pure magic. Use this space to reflect on what brings you joy. These can be the small, simple things that help you stay present in the moment and make you feel grateful for experiencing them.

IDEAS FOR Self-Care

- ☐ Set aside time to read a book for enjoyment
- ☐ Practice deep breathing or meditation for 10 minutes
- ☐ Write a list of 10 things you're grateful for
- ☐ Take a walk outside
- ☐ Declutter a room or workspace
- ☐ Call or text a friend to catch up
- ☐ Cook a special meal
- ☐ Practice yoga or gentle stretching
- ☐ Write a positive affirmation and read it throughout the day
- ☐ Create a relaxing bedtime routine
- ☐ Journal about your thoughts and feelings
- ☐ Set aside time for your favorite hobby
- ☐ Give yourself a compliment
- ☐ Unplug from technology for an hour
- ☐ Listen to your favorite music or a calming playlist
- ☐ Be creative (draw, paint, write, or craft)
- ☐ Spend time with a pet or visit a local animal shelter
- ☐ Read a book or watch a movie that inspires you
- ☐ Explore a new relaxation method, like progressive muscle relaxation
- ☐ Take a power nap or a restorative break
- ☐ Create a vision board or list of personal goals
- ☐ Engage in volunteer activities or community service
- ☐ Enjoy a nourishing snack
- ☐ Explore new hobbies or skills that interest you
- ☐ Connect with nature by visiting a park, beach, or forest
- ☐ Take a relaxing bath or shower
- ☐ Set boundaries to protect your energy and time
- ☐ Establish a morning routine that energizes you
- ☐ Be physically activity (sports, exercise, or outdoor activities)
- ☐ Eat mindfully by paying attention to the flavors/textures of food

SELF-CARE PLANNER

Use this planner to organize and prioritize self-care activities, making it easier to plan and incorporate them into your daily routines.

Monday

WHAT MADE ME HAPPY TODAY:

SELF-CARE ACTIVITIES

WATER INTAKE

TODAY'S MOOD

DAILY NUTRITION:
- Breakfast _____
- Lunch _____
- Dinner _____

HABIT TO START:

HABIT TO STOP:

SELF-CARE PLANNER

Use this planner to organize and prioritize self-care activities, making it easier to plan and incorporate them into your daily routines.

Tuesday

WHAT MADE ME HAPPY TODAY:

SELF-CARE ACTIVITIES

WATER INTAKE

TODAY'S MOOD

DAILY NUTRITION:
- Breakfast _____
- Lunch _____
- Dinner _____

HABIT TO START:

HABIT TO STOP:

SELF-CARE PLANNER

Use this planner to organize and prioritize self-care activities, making it easier to plan and incorporate them into your daily routines.

Wednesday

WHAT MADE ME HAPPY TODAY:

SELF-CARE ACTIVITIES

WATER INTAKE

TODAY'S MOOD

DAILY NUTRITION:
- Breakfast
- Lunch
- Dinner

HABIT TO START:

HABIT TO STOP:

SELF-CARE PLANNER

Use this planner to organize and prioritize self-care activities, making it easier to plan and incorporate them into your daily routines.

Thursday

WHAT MADE ME HAPPY TODAY:

SELF-CARE ACTIVITIES

WATER INTAKE

TODAY'S MOOD

DAILY NUTRITION:
- Breakfast _____
- Lunch _____
- Dinner _____

HABIT TO START:

HABIT TO STOP:

SELF-CARE PLANNER

Use this planner to organize and prioritize self-care activities, making it easier to plan and incorporate them in your daily routines.

Friday

WHAT MADE ME HAPPY TODAY:

SELF-CARE ACTIVITIES

WATER INTAKE

TODAY'S MOOD

DAILY NUTRITION:
- Breakfast _____
- Lunch _____
- Dinner _____

HABIT TO START:

HABIT TO STOP:

SELF-CARE PLANNER

Use this planner to organize and prioritize self-care activities, making it easier to plan and incorporate them in your daily routines.

Saturday

WHAT MADE ME HAPPY TODAY:

SELF-CARE ACTIVITIES

WATER INTAKE

TODAY'S MOOD

DAILY NUTRITION:
- Breakfast _____
- Lunch _____
- Dinner _____

HABIT TO START:

HABIT TO STOP:

SELF-CARE PLANNER

Use this planner to organize and prioritize self-care activities, making it easier to plan and incorporate them in your daily routines.

Sunday

WHAT MADE ME HAPPY TODAY:

SELF-CARE ACTIVITIES

WATER INTAKE

TODAY'S MOOD

DAILY NUTRITION:
- Breakfast _____
- Lunch _____
- Dinner _____

HABIT TO START:

HABIT TO STOP:

POSTIVE SELF TALK

Reflect on your strengths, qualities, and accomplishments that make you unique and valuable. Use positive language and phrases to create a positive mindset. By creating and saying self-affirmations, you can build confidence and resilience and reduce negative thought patterns that take form in your mind. Repeat your affirmations daily or as often as you need.

SAFETY NETWORK

Write the names of support people in your most trusted network, in each layer of the circle. The circle closest to you, would be those that you trust the most. For example, the closest circle may be your parents, and the furthest circle is the police. You can write more than one safety person in each layer.

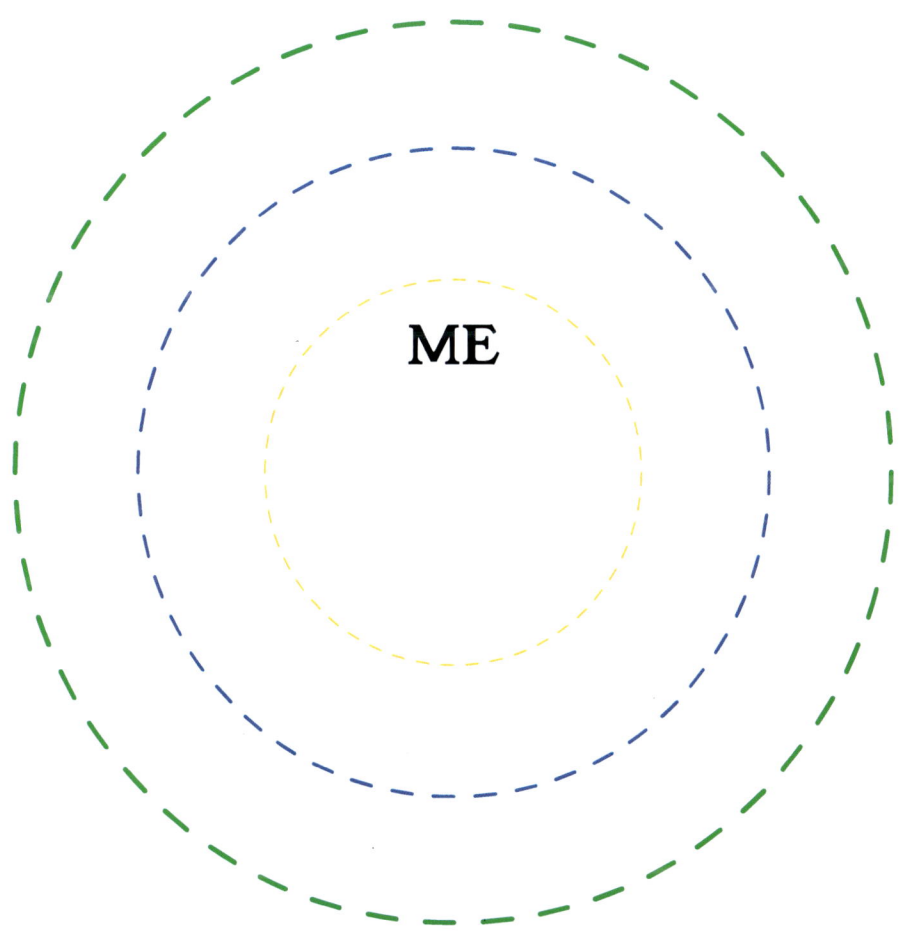

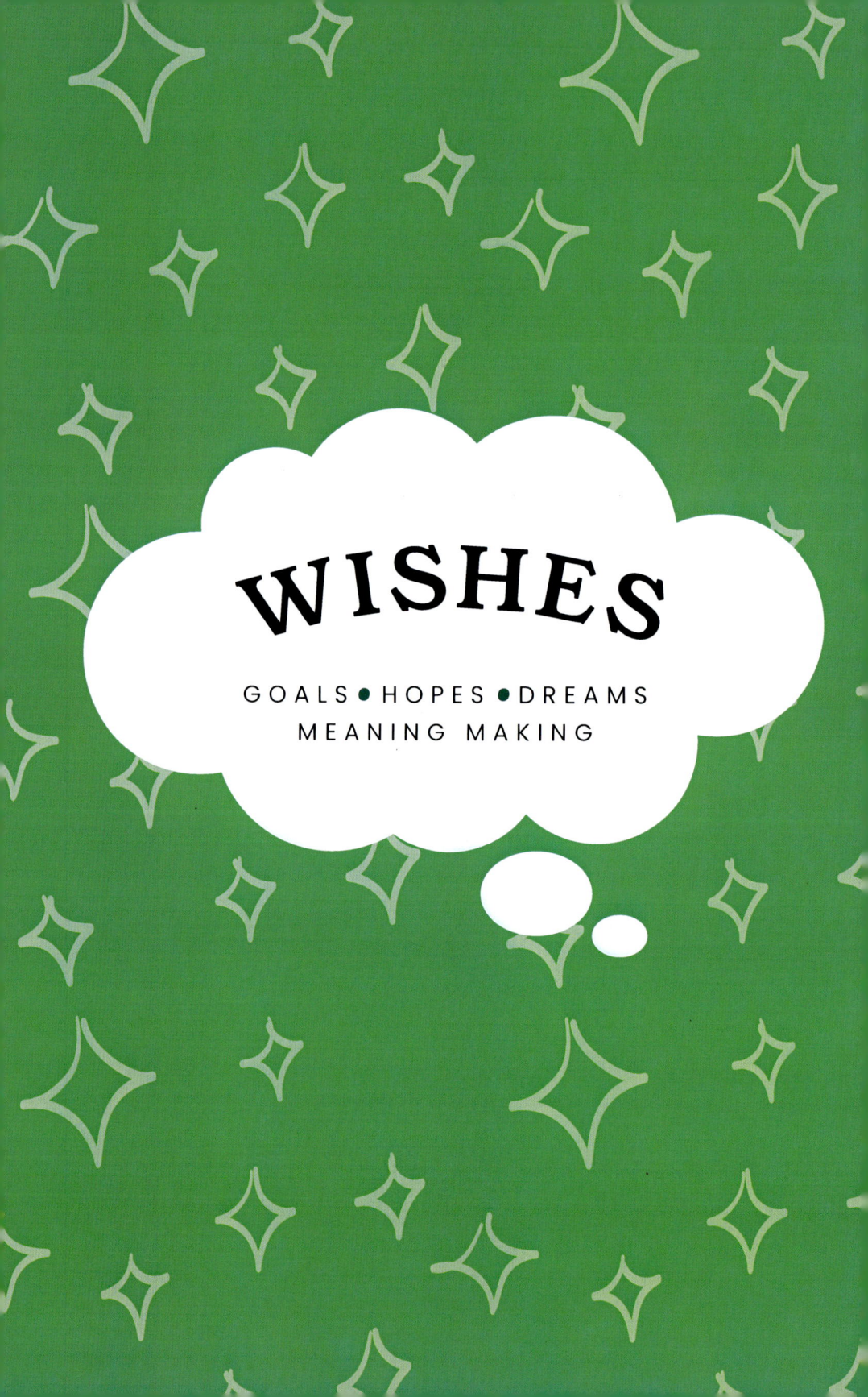

WISHES

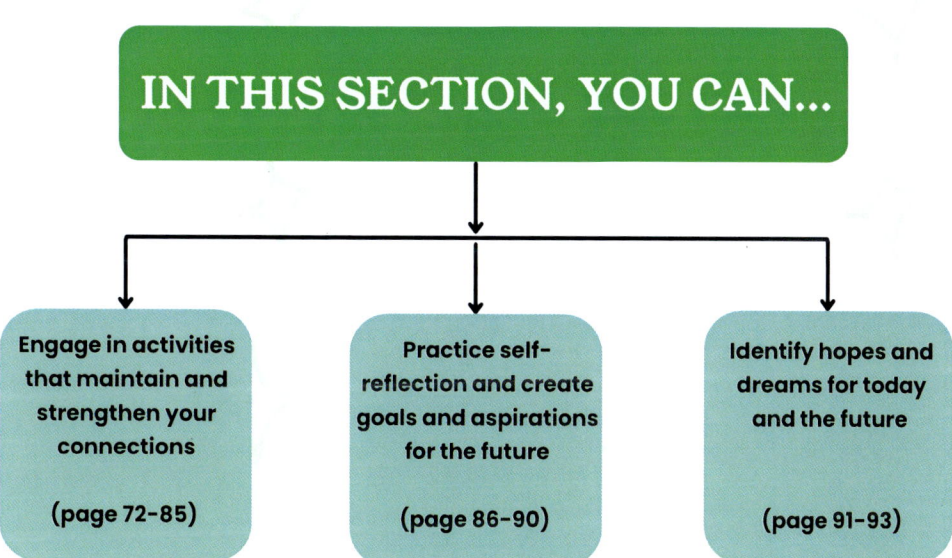

IN THIS SECTION, YOU CAN...

- Engage in activities that maintain and strengthen your connections (page 72-85)
- Practice self-reflection and create goals and aspirations for the future (page 86-90)
- Identify hopes and dreams for today and the future (page 91-93)

WHAT YOU MIGHT NEED

Pencil or Pen · Coloured Pencils · Photos · Craft Materials · Mindful Breaks

SPECIAL DAYS

Identify special days that you wish to celebrate or acknowledge throughout the year. These can be days that help you feel connected to the person who died or days that hold significance to you, like birthdays or holidays. Remember, these days can also be about any special day in any other part of your life that holds meaning to you.

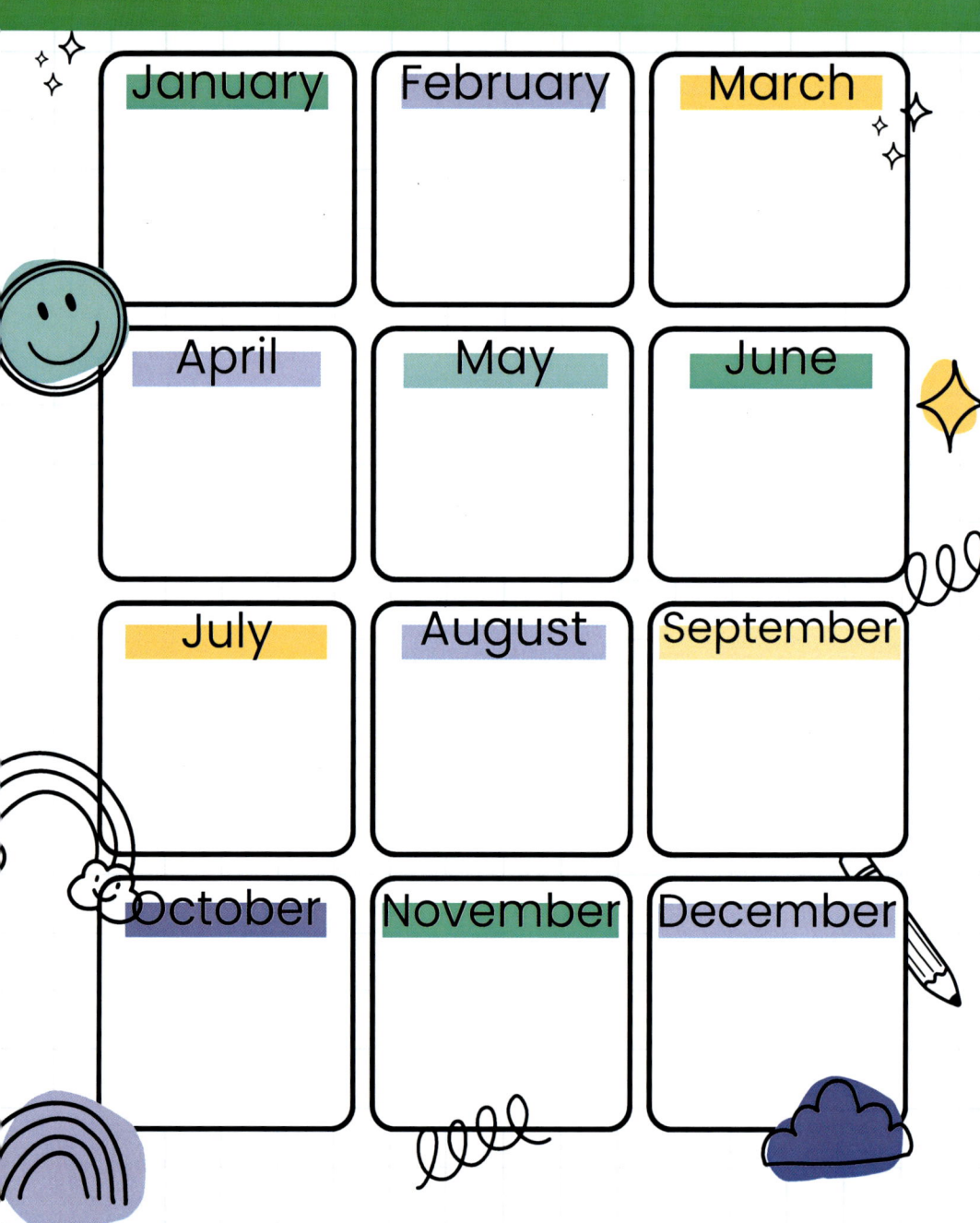

SPECIAL MOMENTS

Draw, write, or cut out and paste pictures of favourite memories you have with the person who died. Use this space to reflect on happy moments that brought you joy and comfort.

PURPOSEFUL PAUSE

When someone dies and is not with us physically, it can feel hard to stay connected and continue the relationship. However, staying connected and maintaining your bond is possible, if this is important to you. If you want to feel connected to someone who has died, there are many ways that you can maintain your special bond and continue to strengthen it - this is called "continuing bonds".

It is important to remember that it is your choice if you want to continue your relationship and just like the changing tides, your choice can change overtime.

CONTINUING BONDS

Continuing bonds activities are meaningful ways to strengthen and maintain a connection with a person who has died. On this page, you will find examples of activities that can help you stay connected to and celebrate the person who has died.

Here are some continuing bond activities that you might find helpful for maintaining your relationship to the person who died:

Establish and participate in celebration of life rituals or traditions that honour your person.	Create photo collages or scrapbooks that capture special moments with your person.	Write letters to your person, sharing thoughts, feelings, and updates on your life.
Cook and eat their favourite meal. Share these meals with friends and family.	Plant flowers in memory of your person.	Create playlists or listen to their favourite music.
Create a memory box and include items that remind you of your person.	Visit special places that were important to your person.	Get involved in activities or hobbies that your person enjoyed doing.

CONTINUING BONDS

Are there other ways to stay connected to your person, or activities that you would want to engage in that are meaningful to you? Use this space to create a list of continuing bond activities.

REMEMBERING YOU

How do you want to remember and celebrate your person? Circle your preferences and then share your answers with friends or family. Many young people say that remembering rituals help them feel relieved and comforted to know that their person won't be forgotten.

Think about who you would like to include in these rituals and how often you would like to engage in them!

THIS OR THAT

Plant a memorial garden.	 OR	Host a memorial gathering with family and friends.
Create a tribute video with video clips, photos, and messages from family and friends.	 OR	Create a memory book filled with photos, notes, and mementos.
Cook or share their favourite meals.	 OR	Frame something they wrote, like a poem or recipe.
Visit places that were special to the person.	 OR	Create a memorial space in your home with pictures and keepsakes.

REMEMBERING ME

After someone you know dies, it is common for young people to wonder about their own death. If you were to die, how do you want people to remember and celebrate you? Create a page of doodles that represent your wishes. Add words or short descriptions to each doodle.

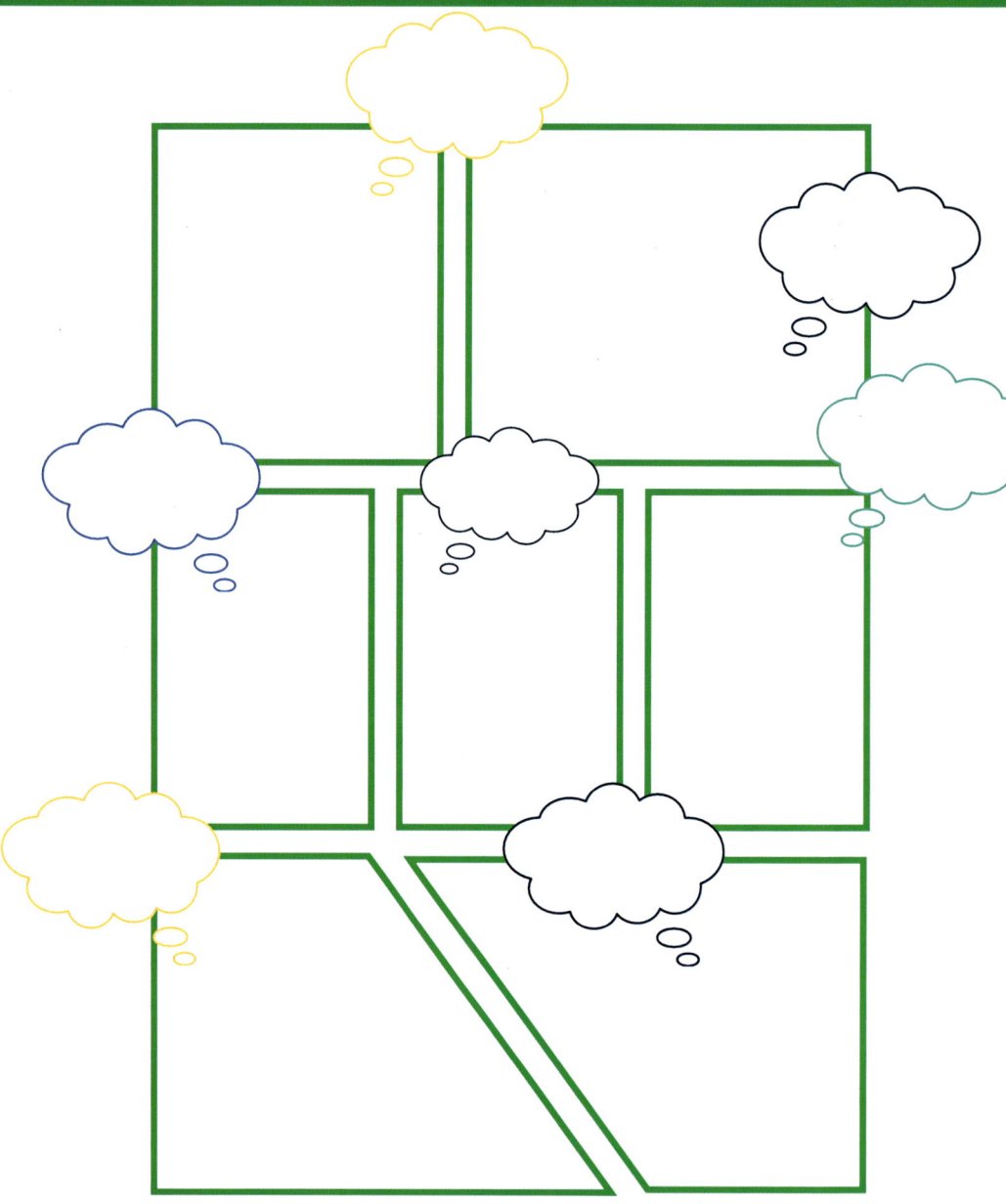

PURPOSEFUL PAUSE

When someone dies, there might be things you wish you said to them or updates that you wish you could give. Writing a letter to the person who has died can be a helpful exercise that allows you to express your thoughts, feelings, memories, and life updates in a personal and meaningful way. It is also a way to create a sense of continuity and connection.

On the following pages, you will have the opportunity to write letters to the person/people who have died. Choose a quiet and comfortable space where you can focus without interruptions. Begin with a simple greeting, and then write to them as if you were talking to them (include memories, unfinished conversations, changes and challenges, accomplishments, and other important updates). You can choose to keep your letters or release them (rip it, bury it, or let it float away in water). There is no right or wrong way to do this exercise. Take as much time as you need, and always know that you can continue to write to your person if it feels right for you.

LETTER WRITING

Dear

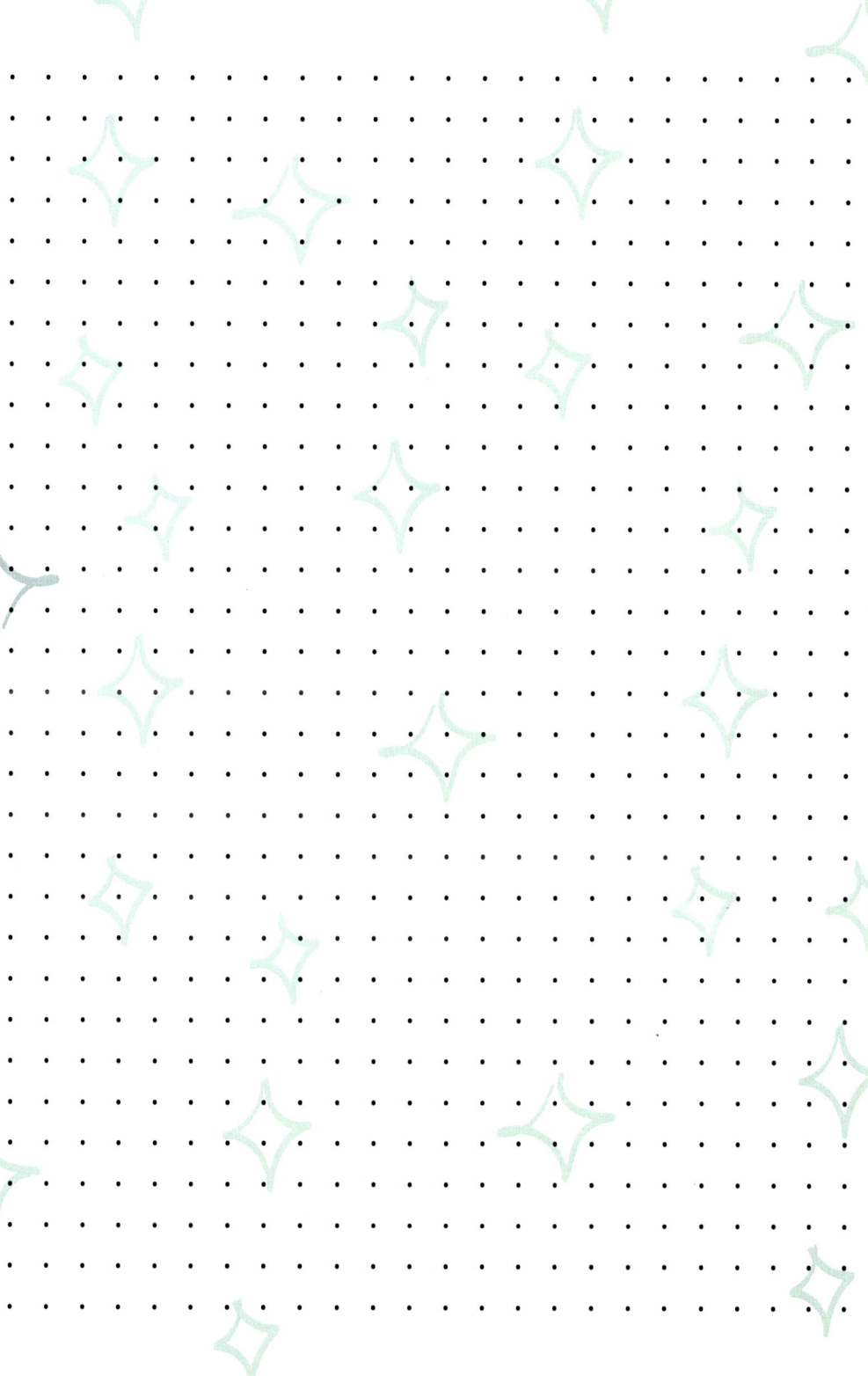

LETTER WRITING

Dear

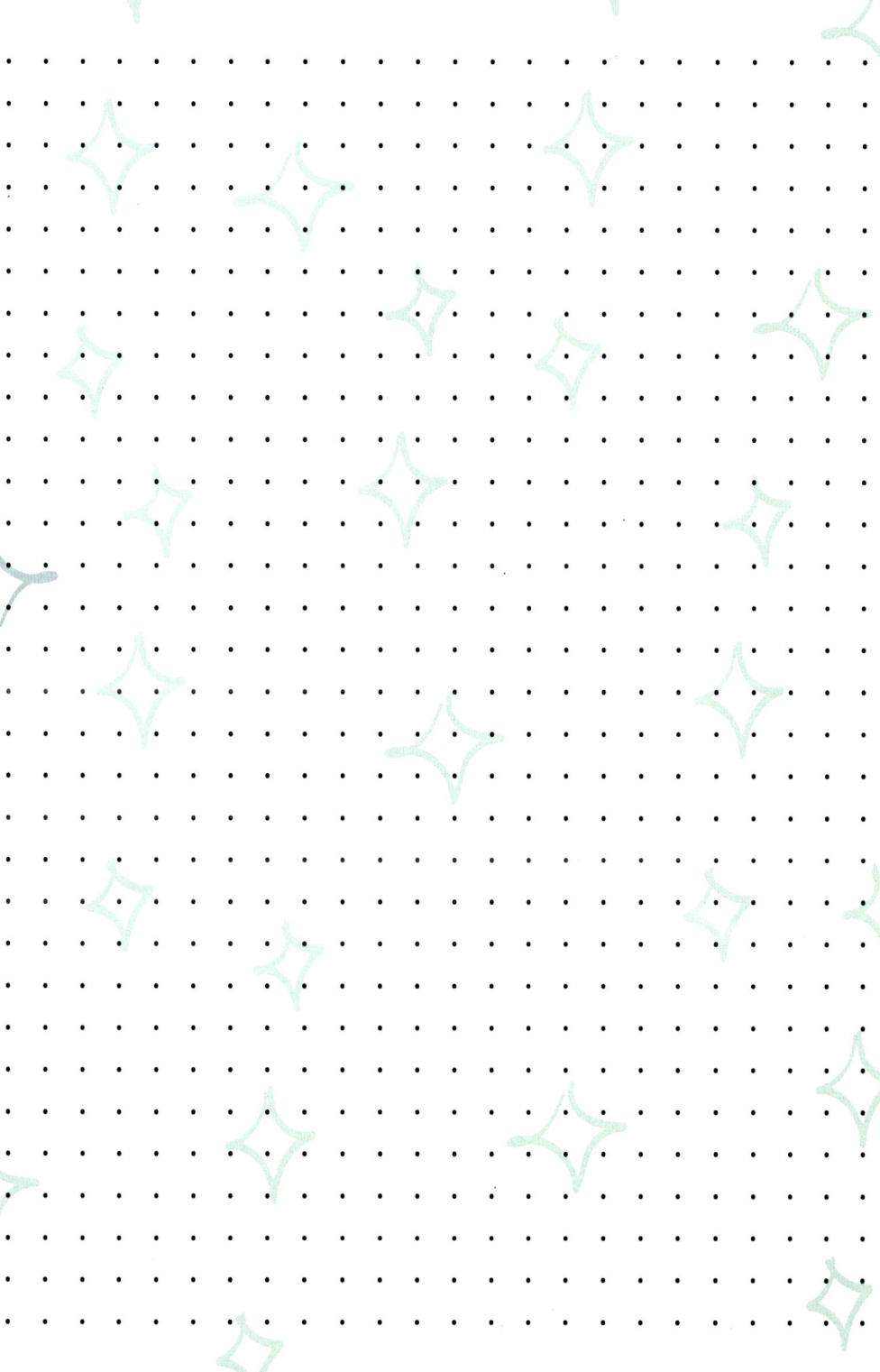

LETTER WRITING

Dear

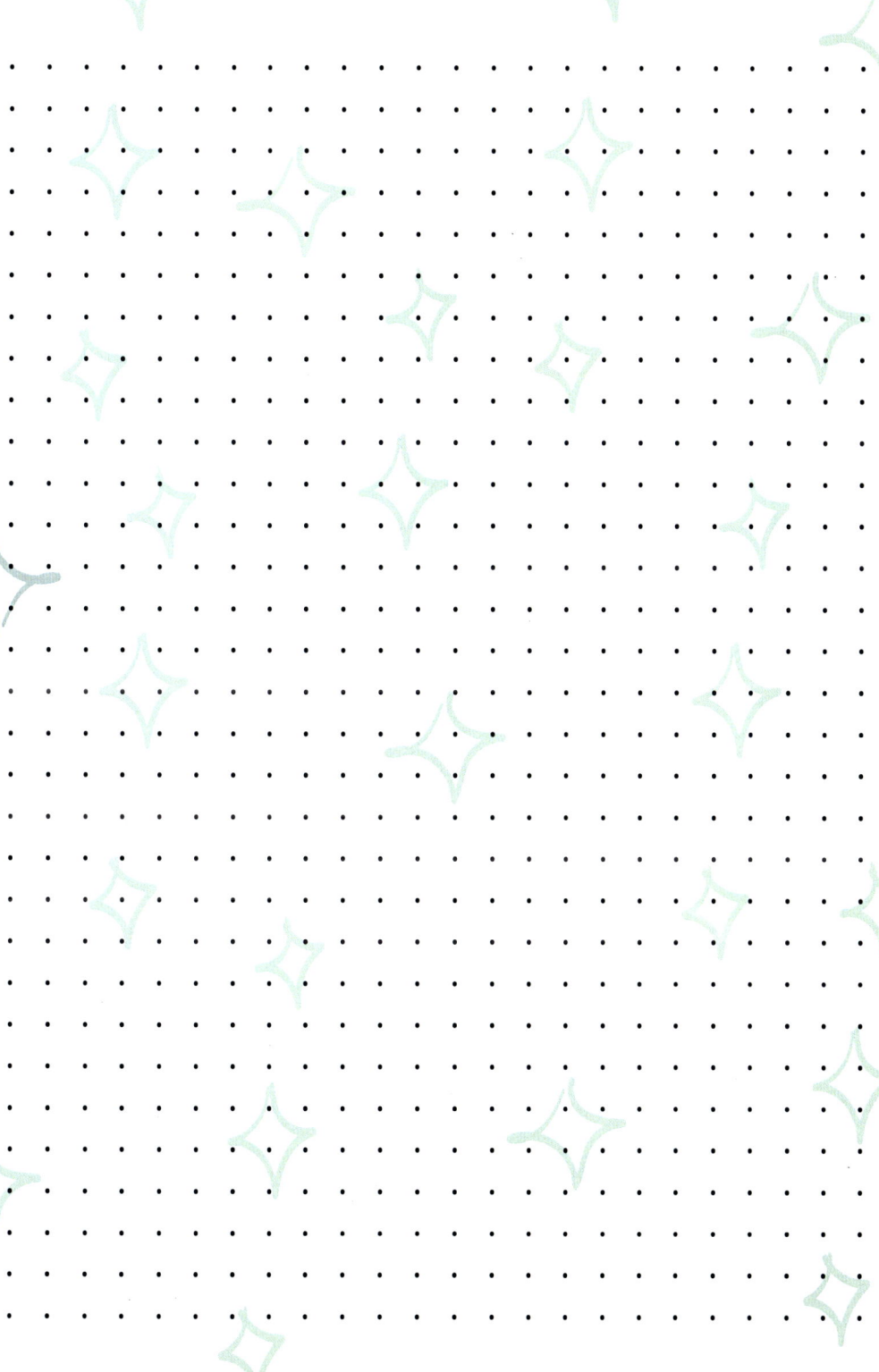

PURPOSEFUL PAUSE

Reflection, goal-setting, and identifying hopes and dreams for the future play an important role in supporting your emotional well-being and personal growth.

When you make time for these activities, you get to process your feelings in a way that makes sense, find meaning in what you are going through, learn how you respond or react to situations, identify coping strategies, know what support is there for you, and start looking ahead with hope and a plan.

Even in the midst of grief, you are allowed to wish, to dream, to imagine, and to achieve greatness. This is your reminder... make a wish and work towards making your dreams come true.

REFLECTION QUESTIONS

Reflection can be a helpful tool for navigating emotions and experiences. Read through these reflection questions and take time to respond to them thoughtfully. Remember, you can keep your reflections to yourself or share them with a trusted person who can offer support and guidance.

- What are my strengths?

- What activities or hobbies bring me joy or offer a positive distraction?

- What do I love about myself?

- What brings me the most joy in life?

- Who and what gives me comfort?

- What support systems do I have in place?

- How can I practice self-compassion?

- What am I grateful for, even in the midst of grief?

- How have my thoughts on life and relationships changed since experiencing grief?

- What is my favorite memory?

WHEEL OF LIFE

Reflection is an important part of understanding more about yourself, what you are experiencing, and the world around you. Reflection can also help to ground you in the present moment. Think about what your life looks like at present. Fill each section of this wheel with words, pictures, or other representations that reflect your current life.

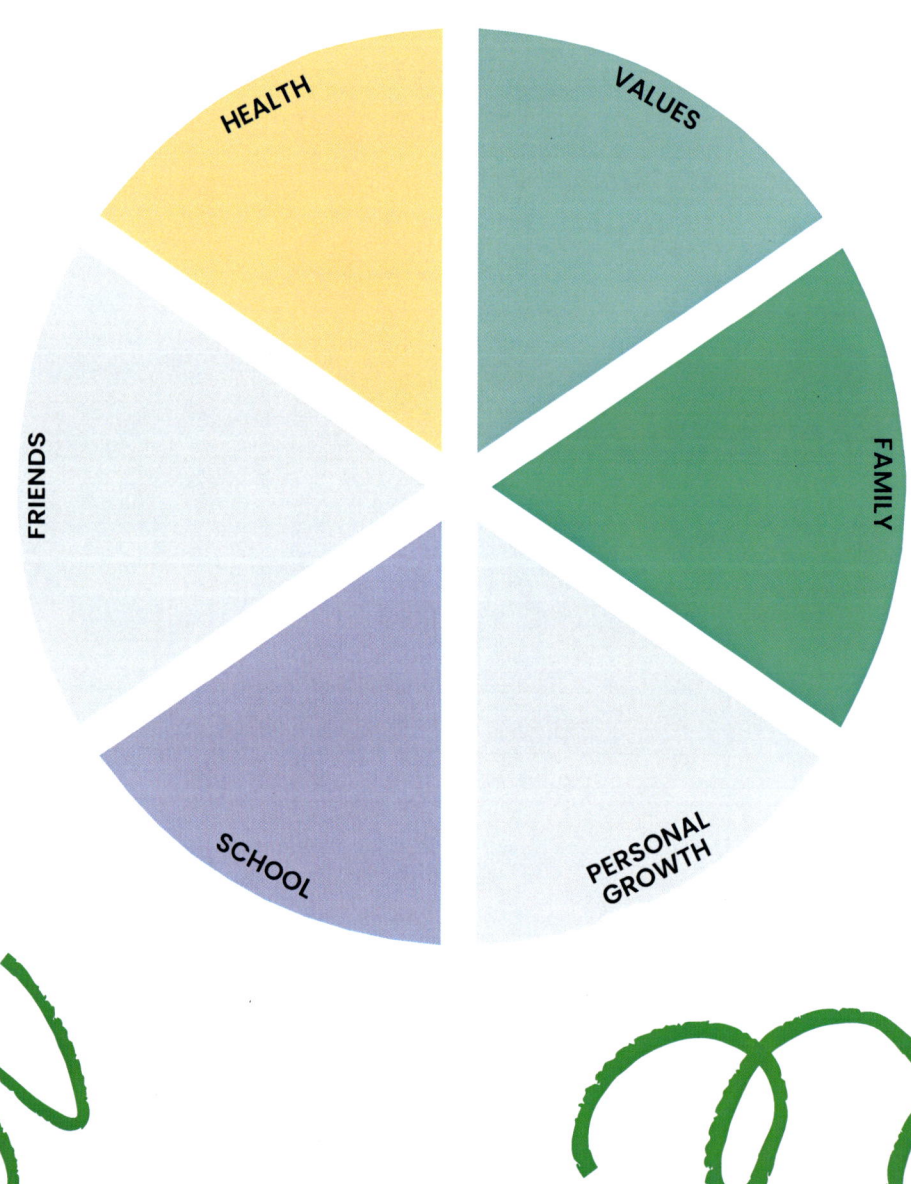

GOALS CHECKLIST

Goal :

Steps :
- ....
- ....
- ....

Why is this goal important?

Goal :

Steps :
- ....
- ....
- ....

Why is this goal important?

Goal :

Steps :
- ....
- ....
- ....

Why is this goal important?

Goal :

Steps :
- ....
- ....
- ....

Why is this goal important?

Goal :

Steps :
- ....
- ....
- ....

Why is this goal important?

SKILL-BUILDING CHALLENGE

Think about trying something new, like learning to play an instrument, painting, or playing a sport. Trying new things can help you express yourself, take your mind off things, and bring you comfort and joy during challenging times. What will your next adventure be?

skills	skills

hobbies	hobbies

WISH JAR

Write down wishes you have and find quotes about dreams that inspire you. Take a moment now, and then look back at your wishes, seeing how far you have come and the progress you have made.

DREAM BOARD

Cut out images or words from magazines to create a collage representing your dreams and wishes. These can be for yourself, your community, or the world. Reflect on each element and why it is meaningful.

A NOTE TO MYSELF

Write a letter to your future self, acknowledging your personal growth as well as detailing your wishes and aspirations. Date the letter and revisit it in 365 days - be sure to set a calendar reminder on a device.

Date written on: _____

Date revisited on: _____

Hey friend,

As you come to the end of this grief notebook, it is important that you take a moment to pat yourself on your back and celebrate how far you have come since first opening up the notebook! Grieving is a journey, a wandering path that never truly ends. Every step you have taken, every page you have filled, is an act of bravery and courage. Here at Upopolis, we see you and are so proud of the strength and resilience, you have shown, especially amid your sorrow and grief.

Opening up this grief notebook was a courageous step. We hope this notebook has been a safe place for you to share your thoughts, feelings, and experiences, as well as a place to learn, grow, and reflect.

Within the pages of this notebook, you have captured so much of your grief journey, including your emotions, the ups, the downs, and everything in between. It is a powerful tool, a companion that will be with you. You are learning to navigate a world that has changed, and with every tear, every laugh, every memory, you're growing around your grief and becoming resilient.

So, our courageous friend, take a deep breath in and exhale, acknowledging the bravery that lives within you. And remember, when your days feel hard and your emotions are big, open your notebook. Let it be a reminder of a piece of your journey, your courage, and the incredible person you are and are becoming.

Keep going, keep growing, and remember that you are never alone.

With care,

The Upopolis Team

POSITIVE AFFIRMATION ANSWER KEY

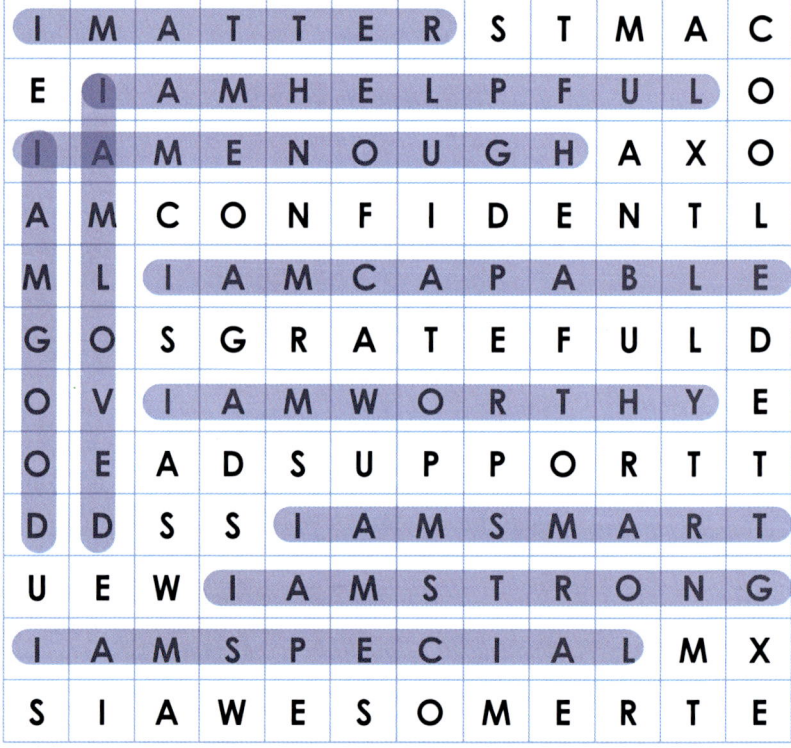